Delicious
lunches

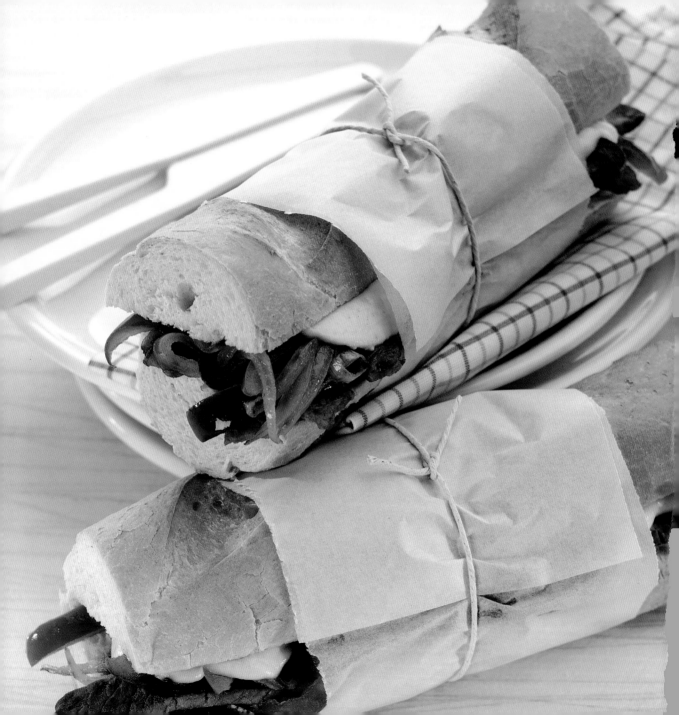

Delicious lunches

Love Food is an imprint of Parragon Books Ltd

Parragon
Queen Street House
4 Queen Street
Bath BA1 1HE

Cover and internal design by Mark Cavanagh
Introduction by Bridget Jones
Photography by Don Last
Additional photography by Gunter Beer
Home Economist Christine Last

ISBN 978-1-4054-9641-4
Printed in China

Notes for reader
• This book uses metric and imperial measurements. Follow the same units of
measurements throughout; do not mix imperial and metric.
• All spoon measurements are level: teaspoons are assumed to be 5 ml and
tablespoons are assumed to be 15 ml.
• Unless otherwise stated, milk is assumed to be low fat and eggs are medium. The
times given are an approximate guide only.
• Some recipes contain nuts. If you are allergic to nuts you should avoid using them
and any products containing nuts. Recipes using raw or very lightly cooked eggs
should be avoided by infants, the elderly, pregnant women, convalescents and anyone
suffering from illness.

Contents

Lunches

There are those who 'lunch' and for whom midday dining is a status symbol in terms of where, rather than what. For most, lunch means everything from an apple at the desk to business meetings, cheese sandwiches to a food fiesta. Snacking or celebrating, lunch is about making the most of an array of eating. Don't miss out – enjoy!

Snack attack

Hunger pangs: no plans, no time and no lunch allowance? It's easy to grab a supermarket snack-pack and fall into the lousy lunch routine. Take a fresh look at lunch-box options for all the family, whatever they may be doing at work, school, during holidays or together for an outing.

• Leafy salads stay fresh when the dressing is packed separately.

• Pasta, potatoes, beans and pulses make good prepare-ahead lunches.

• Crunchy nuts and seeds go well with couscous or rice bases, as well as most other salads.

• Shredded roots and shoots travel well – carrots, celery or beetroot and bean sprouts.

Sandwich world

Sandwiches can be brilliantly good. Keep fillings light, such as canned tuna, lean roast beef, cooked ham, smoked chicken or turkey or finely grated cheese, or have vegetable-based fillings. Delicate open sandwiches with stylish toppings are smart for leisurely lunches.

• Ciabbata, French bread, soft tortilla wraps, light rye, wholemeal or mixed grain, use all breads, not the same each day. Slice them thickly to satisfy appetites with carbohydrate rather than too much fat.

• Cut the fat for everyday eating. Butter isn't always essential and thick-spread mayonnaise or full-fat cream cheese should be a rare treat. Try brushing olive, walnut or pistachio oil lightly over thick breads; use low-fat soft cheese to spread; spread full-flavoured pesto finely; or use peanut (or other nut) butter thinly.

• Include lots of finely cut vegetables – peppers, courgettes, cabbage, tomatoes, cucumber, fennel, celery or carrot.

Just a light bite?

When supper is going to be special, satisfy midday hunger with a combination of light foods and a nutritious drink.

In winter, soups are a good choice. Home-made, they can be reheated rapidly in the microwave. Carry them in a vacuum flask for a warming lunch away from home.

Lunchtime celebrations

Lunch is the perfect time to bring people together for a relaxed celebration that can be smart and slightly formal or simply fun.

• Allow gathering time for everyone to arrive and relax. Provide nibbles merely to whet the appetite. Don't expect guests to leave promptly; plan to round off over lots of afternoon tea.

• Sit-down lunches are unrushed. Linger over and between courses. Plan a menu that will not spoil; include cook-ahead dishes and desserts that go from refrigerator to table.

• Get everyone involved for informal fun: try self-service straight from the kitchen.

Lunch Box

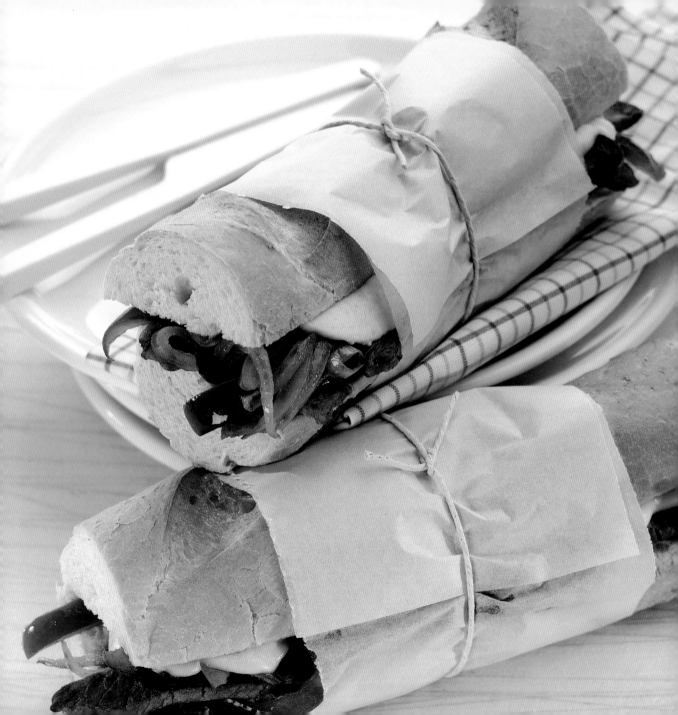

serves 4

1 baguette

350 g/12 oz boneless rib-eye
steak, partially frozen

3 tbsp olive oil

1 onion, thinly sliced

1 green pepper, cored,
deseeded and thinly sliced

salt and pepper

75 g/2¾ oz halloumi
or mozzarella cheese,
thinly sliced

cheese steak baguette

Cut the baguette into 4 equal lengths, then cut each piece in half horizontally. Thinly slice the partially frozen steak across the grain.

Heat 2 tablespoons of the oil in a large frying pan over a medium heat, add the onion and pepper and cook, stirring occasionally, for 10–15 minutes until both vegetables are softened and the onion is golden brown. Push the mixture to one side of the frying pan.

Heat the remaining oil in the frying pan over a medium heat. When hot, add the steak and stir-fry for 4–5 minutes until tender. Stir the onion mixture and steak together and season to taste with salt and pepper.

Preheat the grill to medium. Divide the steak mixture between the 4 bottom halves of bread and top with the cheese. Place them on a grill rack and grill for 1–2 minutes until the cheese has melted, then cover with the top halves of bread and press down gently. Serve immediately, or wrap in greaseproof paper or foil for a packed lunch.

serves 4

1 baguette

butter, for spreading

mixed salad leaves

3 tbsp olive oil

2 onions, thinly sliced

675 g/1 lb 8 oz rump or sirloin steak, about 2.5 cm/
1 in thick

salt and pepper

1 tbsp Worcestershire sauce

2 tbsp wholegrain mustard

2 tbsp water

mustard steak baguette

Cut the bread into 4 equal lengths, then cut each piece horizontally in half. Spread each half with some butter and add a few salad leaves to the bottom halves.

Heat 2 tablespoons of the oil in a large, heavy-based frying pan over a medium heat. Add the onions and cook, stirring occasionally, for 10–15 minutes until softened and golden brown. Using a slotted spoon, transfer to a plate and set aside.

Increase the heat to high and add the remaining oil to the pan. When hot, add the steak, season to taste with pepper and cook quickly on both sides to seal. Reduce the heat to medium and cook, turning once, for 2½–3 minutes each side for rare or 3½–5 minutes each side for medium. Transfer the steak to the plate with the onions.

Add the Worcestershire sauce, mustard and water to the pan and stir to deglaze by scraping any sediment from the base of the pan. Return the onions to the pan, season to taste with salt and pepper and mix well.

Thinly slice the steak across the grain, divide it between the 4 bottom halves of bread and cover with the onions. Cover with the top halves of bread and press down gently. Serve at once or wrap in greaseproof paper or foil for a packed lunch.

serves 4

115 g/4 oz mozzarella
cheese, grated

115 g/4 oz Cheddar cheese,
grated

225 g/8 oz cooked chorizo
sausage (outer casing
removed) or ham, diced

4 spring onions,
finely chopped

2 fresh green chillies, such as
poblano, deseeded and
finely chopped

salt and pepper

8 flour tortillas

vegetable oil, for brushing

guacamole and salsa,
to serve

chorizo & cheese quesadillas

Place the cheeses, chorizo, spring onions, chillies and salt and pepper to taste in a bowl and mix together.

Divide the mixture between 4 of the flour tortillas, then top with the remaining tortillas.

Brush a large, non-stick or heavy-based frying pan with oil and heat over a medium heat. Add 1 quesadilla and cook, pressing it down with a spatula, for 4–5 minutes until the underside is crisp and lightly browned. Turn over and cook the other side until the cheese is melting. Remove from the frying pan and keep warm. Cook the remaining quesadillas.

Cut each quesadilla into quarters, arrange on a warmed serving plate and serve accompanied by some guacamole and salsa. If eating away from the home, wrap the quesadillas in greaseproof paper or foil, and transport the guacamole and salsa in air tight containers.

serves 2

1 tbsp natural yogurt

1 tsp olive oil

$^1/_2$ tsp white wine vinegar

$^1/_2$ tsp Dijon mustard

pepper

1 large egg, hard-boiled
and cooled

200 g/7 oz canned tuna
in spring water, drained

200 g/7 oz canned
no-added-sugar sweetcorn
kernels, drained

2 wholemeal flour tortillas

1 punnet mustard cress

tortillas with tuna, egg & sweetcorn

To make the dressing, whisk the yogurt, oil, vinegar and mustard, and pepper to taste, in a jug until emulsified and smooth.

Shell the egg, separate the yolk and the white, then mash the yolk and chop the white finely. Mash the tuna with the egg and dressing, then mix in the sweetcorn.

Spread the filling equally over the 2 tortillas and sprinkle over the mustard cress. Fold in one end and roll up. Wrap in foil for a packed lunch.

serves 4

85 g/3 oz grated carrot

55 g/2 oz white cabbage,
thinly sliced

85 g/3 oz natural yogurt

1 tsp cider vinegar

25 g/1 oz raisins

200 g/7 oz canned tuna steak
in water, drained

2 tbsp pumpkin seeds

pepper

4 wholemeal or
white pitta breads

4 dessert apples, to serve

raisin coleslaw & tuna-filled pitta breads

Mix the carrot, cabbage, yogurt, vinegar and raisins together in a bowl. Lightly stir in the tuna and half the pumpkin seeds and season to taste with pepper.

Lightly toast the pitta breads under a preheated hot grill or in a toaster, then leave to cool slightly. Using a sharp knife, cut each pitta bread in half. Divide the filling evenly between the pitta breads and sprinkle the remaining pumpkin seeds over the filling. Core the apples and cut into wedges, then serve immediately with the filled pitta breads.

If you are planning on eating this away from the home, prepare the filled pitta breads as described above and wrap well in foil. The apple should be kept whole and cut into wedges just before you plan to eat.

serves 2

2–4 pitta breads

1 tsp vinegar

1/2 tsp Dijon mustard

1/4 iceberg lettuce,
finely shredded

1 spring onion, chopped

1/2 yellow pepper, deseeded
and chopped

1 large tomato, deseeded
and chopped

5-cm/2-inch piece
cucumber, chopped

1 carrot, peeled and grated

for the hummus

400 g/14 oz canned
chickpeas, drained and liquid
reserved

1 garlic clove, chopped

3 tbsp olive oil

2 tbsp tahini

juice of 1/2 lemon

pepper

pinch of paprika

pitta pockets with hummus & salad

To make the hummus, put the chickpeas, garlic, 2 tablespoons of the oil, the tahini, lemon juice and a little of the chickpea liquid in a blender or food processor and blend until smooth and creamy. Season to taste with pepper and the paprika.

If serving at home, heat the pitta breads according to the packet instructions and split each one to create a pocket.

To make the dressing, whisk the remaining oil with the vinegar and mustard, and pepper to taste, in a jug.

Mix all the salad ingredients together in a bowl, add the dressing and toss well to coat. Spread the inside of the pitta pockets with the hummus, fill with the salad and serve. For a lunch box, spread the inside of the unheated pitta pockets with hummus, fill with the undressed salad and wrap well in foil.

serves 4

4 large baking
potatoes, pricked

250 g/9 oz cooked skinless,
boneless chicken
breasts, diced

4 spring onions,
sliced thickly

250 g/9 oz low-fat soft cheese

pepper

mixed salad, to serve

baked potatoes with chicken

Bake the potatoes in a preheated oven, 200°C/400°F/Gas Mark 6, for about 60 minutes, until tender, or cook in a microwave on high power for 12–15 minutes.

Mix the chicken and spring onions with the low-fat soft cheese.

Cut a cross through the top of each potato and squeeze slightly apart. Spoon the chicken filling into the potatoes and season with pepper. Serve with a mixed salad.

If you plan to eat this away from home, bake or cook the potato as described above and leave to cool before wrapping in foil. The filling can also be prepared at home and transported in an air-tight container.

makes 2

4 slices walnut bread or pain
Poilâne, about 1 cm/
1/2 inch thick

4 thin slices cured ham, such
as Bayonne or Parma

2 ripe pears, such as
Conference, peeled, halved,
cored and thinly sliced
lengthways

100 g/3 1/2 oz Roquefort
cheese, very thinly sliced

mixed salad leaves

walnut vinaigrette

pear & roquefort open sandwiches

Preheat the grill to high. Put the bread slices under the grill and toast until crisp, but not brown, on both sides. Do not turn off the grill.

Fold or cut the ham slices to cover each slice of bread, then equally divide the pear slices between them. Lay the cheese slices on top.

Return the open sandwiches to the grill until the cheese melts and bubbles. Mix the salad leaves with the walnut vinaigrette and serve 1 or 2 open sandwiches each with the salad on the side.

If you want to eat this away from the home, perhaps at work, you can prepare this in the same way providing you have access to a toaster. It's not essential that the cheese is melted, so the separate ingredients can be transported in individual air-tight containers.

serves 2

2 leeks

25 g/1 oz butter

125 g/4^1/$_2$ oz grated
Gruyère cheese

2 spring onions,
finely chopped

1 tbsp chopped fresh parsley

salt and pepper

2 fresh bagels

bagels with leeks & cheese

Trim the leeks, discarding the green ends, and split down the middle, leaving the root intact. Wash well to remove any grit and slice finely, discarding the root.

Melt the butter over a low heat in a large sauté pan and add the leeks. Cook, stirring constantly, for 5 minutes, or until the leeks are soft and slightly browned. Leave to cool.

Preheat the grill. Mix together the cooled leeks, grated cheese, spring onions, parsley and salt and pepper to taste. Split the bagels and toast lightly on the bottom. Spread the cheese mixture over the top of each bagel and place under the preheated grill until bubbling and golden brown.

You can eat this away from the home, perhaps at work, if you have access to a toaster. The topping can be prepared at home and transported in an air-tight container. The toasted bagels can be eaten with the topping served room temperature.

serves 2

3 wholemeal bread
muffins, halved

2 tbsp tomato purée

2 tbsp pesto

1 tbsp olive oil

1/2 red onion, thinly sliced

3 mushrooms, sliced

1/2 courgette, thinly sliced

2–3 slices ham or
6 slices salami

100 g/3 1/2 oz grated
Cheddar cheese or 6 slices
mozzarella cheese

cherry tomatoes, to serve
(optional)

mini muffin pizzas

Toast the muffins until golden, then leave to cool.

Mix the tomato purée and pesto together in a small bowl and
spread equally over the muffin halves.

Heat the oil in a non-stick frying pan and then cook the onion,
mushrooms and courgette until soft and beginning to brown.

Preheat the grill to high. Divide the vegetables between the
muffins and top with the ham and then the cheese.

Cook under the grill for 3–4 minutes until the cheese is melted
and browned. Serve hot or cold with cherry tomatoes if desired.
Wrap in foil for a packed lunch.

Lunchtime Specials

serves 4

12 slices French bread or
rustic bread

4 tbsp olive oil

2 garlic cloves, chopped

2 tbsp finely chopped
fresh oregano

salt and pepper

100 g/3 1/2 oz cold roast
chicken, cut into small,
thin slices

4 tomatoes, sliced

12 thin slices of goat's cheese

12 black olives,
stoned and chopped

fresh green salad leaves,
to serve

chicken crostini

Preheat the oven to 180°C/350°F/Gas Mark 4 and the grill to medium. Put the bread under the preheated grill and lightly toast on both sides. Meanwhile, pour the olive oil into a bowl and add the garlic and oregano. Season with salt and pepper and mix well. Remove the toasted bread slices from the grill and brush them on one side only with the oil mixture.

Place the bread slices, oiled sides up, on a baking sheet. Put some sliced chicken on top of each one, followed by a slice of tomato. Divide the slices of goat's cheese between them, then top with the chopped olives. Drizzle over the remaining oil mixture and transfer to the preheated oven. Bake for about 5 minutes, or until the cheese is golden and starting to melt. Remove from the oven and serve with fresh green salad leaves.

serves 4

1 small oval-shaped loaf of
white bread
(ciabatta or bloomer)

125 ml/4 fl oz extra-virgin
olive oil

4 tomatoes

6 leaves fresh basil

salt and pepper

8 black olives, stoned and
chopped (optional)

1 large garlic clove

tomato & basil bruschetta

Cut the bread into 1-cm/½-inch slices. Pour half of the oil into a shallow dish and place the bread in it. Leave for 2–3 minutes, turn and leave for 2 more minutes, or until thoroughly saturated in oil.

Meanwhile, seed and dice the tomatoes and place in a mixing bowl. Tear the basil leaves and sprinkle over the tomatoes. Season with salt and pepper. Add the olives, if using. Pour over the remaining olive oil and leave to marinate.

Preheat the griddle over a medium heat. Cook the bread until golden and crispy on both sides (about 2 minutes on each side). Remove the bread from the griddle and arrange on an attractive serving dish.

Peel the garlic clove and cut in half. Rub the cut edge over the surface of the bruschetta. Top each slice with a spoonful of the tomato mixture and serve.

serves 4

450 g/1 lb best steak mince

4 onions

2–4 garlic cloves, crushed

2–3 tsp grated fresh horseradish or 1–1¹/₂ tbsp creamed horseradish

pepper

8 lean back bacon rashers

2 tbsp sunflower oil

sesame seeded buns, to serve

green salad leaves, to garnish

the ultimate steak & bacon burger

Place the steak mince in a large bowl. Finely grate 1 of the onions and add to the steak mince in the bowl.

Add the garlic, horseradish and pepper to the steak mixture in the bowl. Mix together, then shape into 4 equal-sized burgers. Wrap each burger in 2 rashers of bacon, then cover and leave to chill for 30 minutes.

Preheat the grill to medium-high. Slice the remaining onions. Heat the oil in a frying pan. Add the onions and cook over a medium heat for 8–10 minutes, stirring frequently, until the onions are golden brown. Drain on kitchen paper and keep warm.

Cook the burgers under the hot grill for 3–5 minutes on each side or until cooked to personal preference. Serve inside sesame seeded buns with a spoonful of the fried onions and a green salad garnish.

serves 4

2 tbsp sunflower oil, plus extra for oiling

finely grated rind of 1 lime

1 tbsp lime juice

2 garlic cloves, crushed

1/4 tsp ground coriander

1/4 tsp ground cumin

pinch of sugar

salt and pepper

1 piece rump steak, about 675 g/1 lb 8 oz and 2 cm/3/4 inch thick

4 tortillas

1 avocado

2 tomatoes, thinly sliced

4 tbsp soured cream

4 spring onions, thinly sliced

chopped coriander, to garnish

lime wedges, to serve

grilled steak fajitas

To make the marinade, put the oil, lime rind and juice, garlic, coriander, cumin, sugar and salt and pepper to taste into a large, shallow, non-metallic dish large enough to hold the steak and mix together. Add the steak and turn in the marinade to coat it. Cover and leave to marinate in the refrigerator for 6–8 hours or up to 24 hours, turning occasionally.

When ready to cook, preheat the grill. Using a slotted spoon, remove the steak from the marinade, put onto an oiled grill rack and cook under a medium heat for 5 minutes for rare or 8–10 minutes for medium, turning the steak frequently and basting once or twice with any remaining marinade.

Meanwhile, warm the tortillas according to the instructions on the packet. Peel and slice the avocado.

Thinly slice the steak across the grain and arrange an equal quantity of the slices on one side of each tortilla. Add the tomato and avocado slices, top with a spoonful of soured cream and sprinkle over the spring onions. Fold over and eat at once.

serves 4–8

500 g/1 lb 2 oz large flat mushrooms

2 tbsp oil

1 onion, sliced

1 red pepper, deseeded and sliced

1 green pepper, deseeded and sliced

1 garlic clove, crushed

$1/4$–$1/2$ tsp cayenne pepper

juice and grated rind of 2 limes

2 tsp sugar

1 tsp dried oregano

salt and pepper

8 flour tortillas

salsa, to serve

mushroom fajitas

Cut the mushrooms into strips. Heat the oil in a large, heavy-based frying pan. Add the mushrooms, onion, red and green pepper and garlic and stir-fry for 8–10 minutes, until the vegetables are cooked.

Add the cayenne pepper, lime juice and rind, sugar and oregano. Season to taste with salt and pepper and cook for a further 2 minutes.

Meanwhile, heat the tortillas according to the packet instructions. Divide the mushroom mixture between the warmed tortillas and serve with the salsa.

serves 4–6

85 g/3 oz bulgar wheat

300 g/10½ oz canned red kidney beans, drained and rinsed

300 g/10½ oz canned cannellini beans, drained

1–2 fresh red jalapeño chillies, deseeded and roughly chopped

2–3 garlic cloves

6 spring onions, roughly chopped

1 yellow pepper, deseeded, peeled and chopped

1 tbsp chopped fresh coriander

115 g/4 oz mature Cheddar cheese, grated

salt and pepper

2 tbsp wholemeal flour

1–2 tbsp sunflower oil

1 large tomato, sliced

wholemeal buns

vegetarian chilli burgers

Cook the bulgar wheat in a saucepan of lightly salted water for 12 minutes, or until cooked. Drain and reserve.

Place the beans in a food processor with the chillies, garlic, spring onions, pepper, coriander and half the cheese. Using the pulse button, chop finely. Add to the cooked bulgar wheat with salt and pepper to taste. Mix well, then shape into 4–6 equal-sized burgers. Cover and leave to chill for 1 hour. Coat the burgers in the flour.

Preheat the grill to medium. Heat a heavy-based frying pan and add the oil. When hot, add the burgers and cook over a medium heat for 5–6 minutes on each side or until piping hot.

Place 1–2 slices of tomato on top of each burger and sprinkle with the remaining cheese. Cook under the hot grill for 2–3 minutes, or until the cheese begins to melt. Serve in wholemeal buns.

serves 1

2 large eggs

2 tbsp milk

salt and pepper

40 g/1^1/$_2$ oz butter

1 sprig of fresh flat-leaf
parsley, stem bruised

leaves from 1 sprig of fresh
flat-leaf parsley

1 sprig fresh chervil

2 fresh chives

buttered bread, to serve

mixed herb omelette

Break the eggs into a bowl. Add the milk and salt and pepper to taste, and quickly beat until just blended.

Heat a 20-cm/8-inch omelette pan or frying pan over a medium-high heat until it is very hot and you can feel the heat rising from the surface. Add 30 g/1 oz of the butter and use a fork to rub it over the base and around the sides as it melts.

As soon as the butter stops sizzling, pour in the eggs. Shake the pan forwards and backwards over the heat and use the fork to stir the eggs around the pan in a circular motion. Do not scrape the base of the pan.

As the omelette begins to set, use the fork to push the cooked egg from the edge towards the centre, so the remaining uncooked egg comes in contact with the hot base of the pan. Continue doing this for 3 minutes, or until the omelette looks set on the bottom, but is still slightly runny on top.

Place the herbs in the centre of the omelette. Tilt the pan away from the handle, so the omelette slides towards the edge of the pan. Use the fork to fold the top half of the omelette over the herbs. Slide the omelette onto a plate, then rub the remaining butter over the top and serve with buttered bread. Omelettes are best eaten immediately.

serves 2

for the dough

225 g/8 oz plain flour, plus extra for dusting

1 tsp salt

1 tsp easy-blend dried yeast

1 tbsp olive oil, plus extra for brushing

6 tbsp lukewarm water

for the topping

6 tomatoes, sliced thinly

175 g/6 oz mozzarella cheese, drained and sliced thinly

salt and pepper

2 tbsp fresh basil leaves, shredded

2 tbsp olive oil

cheese & tomato pizza

To make the pizza dough, sift the flour and salt into a bowl and stir in the yeast. Make a well in the centre and pour in the oil and water. Gradually incorporate the dry ingredients into the liquid, using a wooden spoon or floured hands.

Turn out the dough onto a lightly floured surface and knead well for 5 minutes, until smooth and elastic. Return to the clean bowl, cover with lightly oiled clingfilm and set aside to rise in a warm place for about 1 hour, or until doubled in size.

Turn out the dough onto a lightly floured surface and knock back. Knead briefly, then cut it in half and roll out each piece into a round about 5 mm/¼ inch thick. Transfer to a lightly oiled baking sheet and push up the edges with your fingers to form a small rim.

For the topping, arrange the tomato and mozzarella slices alternately over the pizza bases. Season to taste with salt and pepper, sprinkle with the basil and drizzle with the olive oil.

Bake in a preheated oven, 230°C/450°F/Gas Mark 8, for 15–20 minutes, until the crust is crisp and the cheese has melted. Serve immediately.

serves 2

4 slices ciabatta bread, lightly toasted

200 g/7 oz feta cheese

2 tbsp olive oil, plus extra for drizzling

1/2 tsp dried chilli flakes

1 tsp dried oregano

85 g/3 oz rocket leaves, to serve

grilled feta cheese with chilli on ciabatta toast

Preheat the grill to hot. Place the toasted ciabatta slices on a baking tray and cover each with a generous slice of feta cheese. Mix the oil, chilli flakes and oregano together and drizzle evenly over the cheese.

Cook under the preheated grill for 2–3 minutes, or until the cheese begins to melt, and place on serving plates. Drizzle over a little extra oil and serve with rocket leaves.

serves 4

675 g/1 lb 8 oz large potatoes

sunflower, corn or groundnut oil, for deep-frying

salt and pepper

french fries

Peel the potatoes and cut into 8-mm/⅜-inch even-sized fingers. As soon as they are prepared, put them into a large bowl of cold water to prevent discoloration, then leave them to soak for 30 minutes to remove the excess starch.

Drain the potatoes and dry well on a clean tea towel. Heat the oil in a deep-fat fryer or large, heavy-based saucepan to 190°C/375°F. If you do not have a thermometer, test the temperature by dropping a potato finger into the oil. If it sinks, the oil isn't hot enough; if it floats and the oil bubbles around the potato, it is ready. Carefully add a small batch of potatoes to the oil (this is to ensure even cooking and to avoid reducing the temperature of the oil) and deep-fry for 5–6 minutes until soft but not browned. Remove from the oil and drain well on kitchen paper. Leave to cool for at least 5 minutes. Continue to deep-fry the remaining potatoes in the same way, allowing the oil to return to the correct temperature each time.

When ready to serve, reheat the oil to 200°C/400°F. Add the potatoes, in small batches and deep-fry for 2–3 minutes until golden brown. Remove from the oil and drain on kitchen paper. Serve immediately, seasoned to taste with salt and pepper.

Light Lunch

serves 4

3 celery sticks, sliced thinly

1/2 cucumber, sliced thinly

2 spring onions, sliced thinly

250 g/9 oz young
spinach leaves

3 tbsp chopped fresh parsley

350g/12 oz boneless,
roast chicken, sliced thinly

smoked almonds, to garnish

for the dressing

2.5-cm/1-inch piece of fresh
root ginger, grated finely

3 tbsp olive oil

1 tbsp white wine vinegar

1 tbsp clear honey

1/2 tsp ground cinnamon

salt and pepper

chicken & spinach salad

Toss the celery, cucumber and spring onions in a large bowl with the spinach leaves and parsley.

Transfer the salad to serving plates and arrange the chicken on top.

In a screw-top jar, combine all the dressing ingredients, including salt and pepper to taste, and shake well to mix. Pour the dressing over the salad. Garnish with a few smoked almonds.

serves 4

750 g/1 lb 10 oz beef fillet, trimmed of any visible fat

1 tsp pepper

2 tsp Worcestershire sauce

3 tbsp olive oil

400 g/14 oz green beans

100 g/3$^{1}/_{2}$ oz small pasta, such as orecchiette

2 red onions, finely sliced

1 large head radicchio

50 g/1$^{3}/_{4}$ oz green olives, stoned

50 g/1$^{3}/_{4}$ oz shelled hazelnuts, whole

for the dressing

1 tsp Dijon mustard

2 tbsp white wine vinegar

5 tbsp olive oil

roast beef salad

Preheat the oven to 220°C/425°F/Gas Mark 7. Rub the beef with pepper to taste and Worcestershire sauce. Heat 2 tablespoons of the oil in a small roasting tin over a high heat, add the beef and sear on all sides. Transfer the dish to the preheated oven and roast for 30 minutes. Remove and leave to cool.

Bring a large saucepan of water to the boil, add the beans and cook for 5 minutes, or until just tender. Remove with a slotted spoon and refresh the beans under cold running water. Drain and put into a large bowl.

Return the bean cooking water to the boil, add the pasta and cook for 11 minutes, or until tender. Drain, return to the saucepan and toss with the remaining oil.

Add the pasta to the beans with the onions, radicchio leaves, olives and hazelnuts. Transfer to a serving dish or salad bowl and arrange some thinly sliced beef on top.

Whisk the dressing ingredients together in a separate bowl, then pour over the salad and serve immediately.

serves 2

100 g/3½ oz small
wholewheat pasta

2 tbsp olive oil,
plus extra if needed

1 tbsp mayonnaise

1 tbsp natural yogurt

2 tbsp pesto

salt and pepper

200 g/7 oz canned tuna
in spring water, drained
and flaked

200 g/7 oz canned
no-added-sugar sweetcorn
kernels, drained

2 tomatoes, peeled, deseeded
and chopped

½ green pepper, deseeded
and chopped

½ avocado, stoned, peeled
and chopped

pasta salad

Cook the pasta in a large saucepan of boiling water for
8–10 minutes until only just tender. Drain, return to the
saucepan and add half the oil. Toss well to coat, then cover
and leave to cool.

Whisk the mayonnaise, yogurt and pesto together in a jug,
adding a little oil if needed to achieve the desired consistency.
Add a pinch of salt and season to taste with pepper.

Mix the cooled pasta with the tuna, sweetcorn, tomatoes, green
pepper and avocado, add the dressing and toss well to coat.

serves 4–6

2 tuna steaks, about 2 cm/
3/4 inch thick

olive oil

salt and pepper

250 g/9 oz green beans,
topped and tailed

garlic vinaigrette

2 hearts of lettuce, leaves
separated

3 large hard-boiled eggs,
quartered

2 juicy vine-ripened
tomatoes, cut into wedges

50 g/13/4 oz anchovy fillets in
oil, drained

55 g/2 oz Niçoise olives

salad niçoise

Heat a ridged cast-iron griddle pan over a high heat until you can feel the heat rising from the surface. Brush the tuna steaks with oil on one side, place oiled-side down on the hot pan and chargrill for 2 minutes.

Lightly brush the top side of the tuna steaks with a little more oil. Use a pair of tongs to turn the tuna steaks over, then season to taste with salt and pepper. Continue chargrilling for a further 2 minutes for rare or up to 4 minutes for well done. Leave to cool.

Meanwhile, bring a saucepan of salted water to the boil. Add the beans to the pan and return to the boil, then boil for 3 minutes, or until tender-crisp. Drain the beans and immediately transfer them to a large bowl. Pour over the garlic vinaigrette and stir together, then leave the beans to cool in the dressing.

To serve, line a platter with lettuce leaves. Lift the beans out of the bowl, leaving the excess dressing behind, and pile them in the centre of the platter. Break the tuna into large flakes and arrange it over the beans.

Arrange the hard-boiled eggs and tomatoes around the side. Place the anchovy fillets over the salad, then scatter with the olives. Drizzle the remaining dressing in the bowl over everything.

serves 4

2 ripe beef tomatoes

150 g/5¹/2 oz fresh
mozzarella cheese

2 avocados

few fresh basil leaves,
torn into pieces

20 black olives

for the dressing

4 tbsp olive oil

1¹/2 tbsp white wine vinegar

1 tsp coarse grain mustard

salt and pepper

tomato, mozzarella & avocado salad

Using a sharp knife, cut the tomatoes into thick wedges
and place in a large serving dish. Drain the mozzarella cheese
and roughly tear into pieces. Cut the avocados in half and
remove the stones. Cut the flesh into slices, then arrange
the mozzarella cheese and avocado with the tomatoes.

Mix the oil, vinegar and mustard together in a small bowl,
add salt and pepper to taste, then drizzle over the salad.

Scatter the basil and olives over the top and serve immediately.

serves 4

4 tomatoes, cut into wedges

1 onion, sliced

1/2 cucumber, sliced

225 g/8 oz olives, stoned

225 g/8 oz feta cheese, cubed
(drained weight)

2 tbsp fresh coriander leaves

fresh flat-leaf parsley

pitta bread, to serve

for the dressing

5 tbsp extra-virgin olive oil

2 tbsp white wine vinegar

1 tbsp lemon juice

1/2 tsp sugar

1 tbsp chopped fresh
coriander

salt and pepper

greek salad

To make the dressing, place the oil, vinegar, lemon juice, sugar
and coriander in a large bowl. Season with salt and pepper and
mix together well.

Add the tomatoes, onion, cucumber, olives, feta cheese and
coriander. Toss all the ingredients together, then divide between
individual serving bowls. Garnish with fresh parsley and serve
with pitta bread.

serves 4

1 large cos lettuce or 2 Little
Gem lettuces

4 canned anchovies in oil,
drained and halved
lengthways

Parmesan shavings,
to garnish

for the dressing

2 garlic cloves, crushed

1¹/₂ tsp Dijon mustard

1 tsp Worcestershire sauce

4 canned anchovies in olive
oil, drained and chopped

1 egg yolk

1 tbsp lemon juice

salt and pepper

150 ml/5 fl oz olive oil

4 tbsp Parmesan cheese
shavings

for the croûtons

4 thick slices day-old bread

2 tbsp olive oil

1 garlic clove, crushed

caesar salad

Preheat the oven to 180°C/350°F/Gas Mark 4. To make the
dressing, place the garlic, mustard, Worcestershire sauce,
anchovies, egg yolk, lemon juice and salt and pepper to taste
in a food processor or blender and process for 30 seconds until
foaming. With the machine still running, add the olive oil, drop
by drop, until the mixture begins to thicken. Continue adding
the oil in a steady stream until all the oil has been incorporated.
Transfer to a bowl. Add a little hot water if the dressing is too
thick. Stir in the Parmesan cheese shavings. Season to taste with
salt and pepper and chill until required.

For the croûtons, cut the bread into 1-cm/¹/₂-inch cubes. Toss
with the oil and garlic in a bowl. Spread out on a baking sheet
in a single layer. Bake in the preheated oven for 15–20 minutes,
stirring occasionally, until browned and crisp. Remove from the
oven and leave to cool.

Separate the lettuce into individual leaves and wash and spin
dry in a salad spinner or pat dry on kitchen paper. (Excess
moisture will dilute the dressing.) Transfer to a polythene bag
and place in the refrigerator.

To assemble the salad, tear the lettuce into pieces and place in
a large serving bowl. Add the dressing and toss well. Top with
the halved anchovies, croûtons and Parmesan cheese shavings.
Serve immediately.

serves 4

12 slices French bread

175 g/6 oz round goat's cheese in a log, cut into 12 slices

125 g/4¹/₂ oz mixed salad leaves, large ones torn into bite-sized pieces

2 tbsp snipped fresh chives

6 tbsp vinaigrette or garlic vinaigrette

pepper

grilled goat's cheese salad

Preheat the grill to high. Place the bread slices on a grill rack and toast until crisp and golden, but not dark brown. Immediately remove the grill rack from under the grill and turn the slices of toast over.

Place a slice of goat's cheese on each bread slice, then return them to the grill and grill for 2 minutes, or until the cheese is golden and bubbling.

Meanwhile, place the salad leaves in a large bowl with the chives, add the dressing of choice and use your hands to toss until the leaves are coated.

Divide the salad between individual plates, top each with 3 cheese-topped toasts and serve while still hot, seasoned with black pepper to taste.

serves 6

6 plum tomatoes, halved

1 red onion, cut into wedges

1 onion, cut into wedges

2 small courgettes,
cut into chunks

1 aubergine, cut into chunks

1 red pepper, deseeded and
thickly sliced

5 tbsp olive oil

few fresh rosemary sprigs

few fresh thyme sprigs

1 tbsp rock salt

pepper

2 large tomatoes,
roughly chopped

crusty bread, to serve

roasted tomatoes with vegetables

Preheat the oven to 200°C/400°F/Gas Mark 6. Place all the plum tomatoes and vegetables in a large baking tray and drizzle with oil.

Arrange the herbs on top, reserving one sprig of thyme for a garnish, and cook in the oven for 20–30 minutes. Toss the vegetables halfway through to coat with the oil. Season to taste with rock salt and pepper and cook for a further 15–20 minutes, until the vegetables are tender and browned.

Remove the baking tray from the oven, stir in the chopped tomatoes, garnish with the remaining thyme and serve immediately with crusty bread.

serves 4

140 g/5 oz long-grain white
or brown rice

4 large red peppers

2 tbsp olive oil

1 garlic clove, chopped

4 shallots, chopped

1 celery stick, chopped

3 tbsp chopped
toasted walnuts

2 tomatoes, peeled
and chopped

1 tbsp lemon juice

50 g/1¾ oz raisins

4 tbsp freshly grated
Cheddar cheese

2 tbsp chopped fresh basil

salt and pepper

fresh basil sprigs, to garnish

lemon wedges, to serve

stuffed red peppers with basil

Preheat the oven to 180°C/350°F/Gas Mark 4. Cook the rice in a saucepan of lightly salted boiling water for 20 minutes if using white rice, or 35 minutes if using brown. Drain, rinse under cold running water, then drain again.

Using a sharp knife, cut the tops off the peppers and reserve. Remove the seeds and white cores, then blanch the peppers and reserved tops in boiling water for 2 minutes. Remove from the heat and drain well. Heat half the oil in a large frying pan. Add the garlic and shallots and cook, stirring, for 3 minutes. Add the celery, walnuts, tomatoes, lemon juice and raisins and cook for a further 5 minutes. Remove from the heat and stir in the cheese, chopped basil and seasoning.

Stuff the peppers with the rice mixture and arrange them in a baking dish. Place the tops on the peppers, drizzle over the remaining oil, loosely cover with foil and bake in the preheated oven for 45 minutes. Remove from the oven. Garnish with basil sprigs and serve with lemon wedges.

4

Ladies who Lunch

serves 4

4 boneless chicken breasts,
about 175 g/6 oz each

salt and pepper

30 g/1 oz unsalted butter

1 tbsp sunflower oil

for the tarragon sauce

2 tbsp tarragon-flavoured
vinegar

6 tbsp dry white wine, such
as Muscadet

250 ml/9 fl oz chicken stock

4 sprigs fresh tarragon, plus
2 tbsp chopped fresh tarragon

300 ml/10 fl oz crème fraîche
or double cream

new potatoes, to serve

chicken in tarragon sauce

Preheat the oven to 190°C/375°F/Gas Mark 5. Season the chicken breasts on both sides with salt and pepper.

Melt the butter with the oil in a sauté or frying pan, large enough to hold the chicken pieces in a single layer, over a medium-high heat. Add the chicken breasts, skin-side down, and fry for 3–5 minutes until golden brown.

Transfer the chicken breasts to a roasting tin and roast for 15–20 minutes, or until they are tender and the juices run clear when a skewer is inserted into the thickest part of the meat. Transfer the chicken to a serving platter, cover with foil, shiny-side down, and set aside.

To make the tarragon sauce, tilt the roasting tin and use a large metal spoon to remove the excess fat from the surface of the cooking juices. Place the roasting tin over a medium-high heat and add the vinegar, scraping any sediment from the base of the tin. Pour in the wine and bring to the boil, still stirring and scraping, and boil until the liquid is reduced by half.

Stir in the stock and whole tarragon sprigs and continue boiling until the liquid reduces to about 125 ml/4 fl oz.

Stir in the crème fraîche and continue boiling to reduce all the liquid by half. Discard the tarragon sprigs, and adjust the seasoning if necessary. Stir the chopped tarragon into the sauce.

Slice the chicken breasts on individual plates and spoon a quarter of the sauce over each. Serve with freshly cooked new potatoes.

serves 4

4 rump, sirloin or fillet
steaks, about 175–225 g/
6–8 oz each and 2.5 cm/
1 inch thick

pepper

olive or sunflower oil,
for shallow-frying

butter, for shallow-frying

for the béarnaise sauce

4 tbsp white wine or
tarragon vinegar

1 shallot, finely chopped

2 fresh tarragon sprigs, plus
1 tbsp finely chopped
fresh tarragon

2 egg yolks

85 g/3 oz butter, softened

salt and pepper

French fries (see page 51) and
crispy onion rings, to serve

pan-fried steaks with béarnaise sauce

First make the sauce. Put the vinegar, shallot and tarragon sprigs into a small, heavy-based saucepan over a medium-low heat and simmer until reduced to 1 tablespoon. Leave to cool.

Strain the cooled vinegar mixture into a double saucepan or a heatproof bowl set over a saucepan of simmering water. Add the egg yolks and whisk together until thick.

Gradually add the butter in small pieces, whisking after each addition, until combined and the sauce has thickened. Add the chopped tarragon and season to taste with salt and pepper.

Cover the surface of the sauce with a piece of dampened greaseproof paper to prevent a skin from forming. Remove from the heat, but leave over the saucepan of hot water to keep hot while you cook the steaks.

Season the steaks to taste with pepper. Heat a film of oil in a large, heavy-based frying pan over a high heat. When hot, add a knob of butter, and as soon as it has melted, add the steaks. Cook quickly on both sides to seal, then reduce the heat to medium and cook, turning once, for 2½–3 minutes each side for rare, 3½–5 minutes each side for medium and 5–7 minutes each side for well done.

Serve the steaks at once, with the Béarnaise sauce, French fries and crispy onion rings.

serves 4

275 g/9³/4 oz fresh baby spinach leaves

2 tbsp olive oil

150 g/5¹/2 oz pancetta cubetti

280 g/10 oz mixed wild mushrooms, sliced

for the dressing

5 tbsp olive oil

1 tbsp balsamic vinegar

1 tsp Dijon mustard

pinch of sugar

salt and pepper

warm mushroom, spinach & pancetta salad

To make the dressing, place the olive oil, vinegar, mustard, sugar, salt and pepper in a small bowl and whisk together.

Rinse the baby spinach under cold running water, then drain and place in a large salad bowl.

Heat the oil in a large frying pan. Add the pancetta and fry for 3 minutes. Add the mushrooms and cook for 3–4 minutes, or until tender.

Pour the dressing into the frying pan and immediately turn the fried mixture and dressing into the bowl with the spinach. Toss until coated with the dressing and serve immediately.

serves 4

1 aubergine

salt and pepper

4–8 lamb chops

3 tbsp olive oil

1 onion, chopped roughly

1 garlic clove, chopped finely

400 g/14 oz canned chopped tomatoes in juice

pinch of sugar

16 black olives, stoned and chopped roughly

1 tsp chopped fresh herbs such as basil, flat-leaf parsley or oregano

lamb with aubergine

Cut the aubergine into 2-cm/¾-inch cubes, put in a colander standing over a large plate, and sprinkle each layer with salt. Cover with a plate and place a heavy weight on top. Leave for 30 minutes to degorge.

Preheat the grill. Rinse the aubergine slices under cold running water, then pat dry with kitchen paper. Season the lamb chops with pepper.

Place the lamb chops on the grill pan and cook under a medium heat for 10–15 minutes until tender, turning once during the cooking time.

Meanwhile, heat the olive oil in a saucepan, add the aubergine, onion and garlic and fry for 10 minutes, until softened and starting to brown. Add the tomatoes and their juice, the sugar, olives, chopped herbs, salt and pepper and simmer for 5–10 minutes.

To serve, spoon the sauce onto 4 warmed serving plates and top with the lamb chops.

serves 4

4 salmon fillets, about
200 g/7 oz each

125 ml/4 fl oz teriyaki
marinade

1 shallot, sliced

2-cm/³⁄4-inch piece fresh
root ginger, finely chopped

2 carrots, sliced

115 g/4 oz closed-cup
mushrooms, sliced

1.2 litres/2 pints
vegetable stock

250 g/9 oz dried medium
egg noodles

115 g/4 oz frozen peas

175 g/6 oz Chinese leaves,
shredded

4 spring onions, sliced

teriyaki salmon fillets with chinese noodles

Wipe off any scales from the salmon skin. Arrange the salmon fillets, skin-side up, in a dish just large enough to fit them in a single layer. Mix the teriyaki marinade with the shallot and ginger in a small bowl and pour over the salmon. Cover and leave to marinate in the refrigerator for at least 1 hour, turning the salmon over halfway through the marinating time.

Put the carrots, mushrooms and stock into a large saucepan. Arrange the salmon, skin-side down, on a shallow baking tray. Pour the fish marinade into the saucepan of vegetables and stock and bring to the boil. Reduce the heat, cover and simmer for 10 minutes.

Meanwhile, preheat the grill to medium. Cook the salmon under the preheated grill for 10–15 minutes, depending on the thickness of the fillets, until the flesh turns pink and flakes easily. Remove from the grill and keep warm.

Add the noodles and peas to the stock and return to the boil. Reduce the heat, cover and simmer for 5 minutes, or until the noodles are tender. Stir in the Chinese leaves and spring onions and heat through for 1 minute.

Carefully drain off 300 ml/10 fl oz of the stock into a small heatproof jug and reserve. Drain and discard the remaining stock. Divide the noodles and vegetables between 4 warmed serving bowls and top each with a salmon fillet. Pour the reserved stock over each meal and serve immediately.

serves 4

1 tbsp each dried thyme,
dried rosemary, dried
oregano and mild paprika

1 tsp garlic powder

2 tsp cumin seeds

1 tbsp sea salt

4 salmon fillets,
skin removed

1 tbsp vegetable oil

150 g/5½ oz baby spinach

for the hollandaise sauce

3 egg yolks

200 g/7 oz butter

1 tbsp lemon juice

pepper

seared salmon with quick hollandaise sauce & baby spinach

Combine the dried herbs, paprika, garlic powder, cumin
seeds and sea salt in a small grinder and process until smooth.
Alternatively, grind by hand using a pestle in a mortar. Rub
1 tablespoon of the mixture into the top of each of the
salmon fillets.

Heat the oil in a large frying pan and cook the salmon, spice-side
down, for 2–3 minutes, or until golden brown. Turn over and
continue cooking until the salmon is cooked to your liking.
Do not overcook or the salmon will be dry.

To make the hollandaise sauce, place the egg yolks in a blender
or food processor. Melt the butter in a small saucepan until
bubbling. With the motor running, gradually add the hot butter
in a steady stream until the sauce is thick and creamy. Add the
lemon juice, and a little warm water if the sauce is too thick,
then season to taste with pepper. Remove from the blender or
food processor and keep warm.

Divide the baby spinach equally between 4 plates, place
the cooked salmon on top and spoon over the sauce. Serve
immediately.

serves 4

4 fresh tuna steaks, about
2-cm/^{3}/$_4$-inch thick

olive oil

salt and pepper

for the green sauce

55 g/2 oz fresh flat-leaf
parsley, leaves and stems

4 spring onions, chopped

2 garlic cloves, chopped

3 anchovy fillets in oil,
drained

30 g/1 oz fresh basil leaves

^{1}/$_2$ tbsp capers in brine,
rinsed and dried

2 sprigs of fresh oregano or
^{1}/$_2$ tsp dried oregano

125 ml/4 fl oz extra-virgin
olive oil

1–2 tbsp lemon juice, to taste

tuna with green sauce

To make the green sauce, put the parsley, spring onions, garlic, anchovy fillets, basil, capers and oregano in a food processor. Pulse to chop and blend together. With the motor still running, pour in the oil through the feed tube. Add lemon juice to taste, then whizz again. If the sauce is too thick, add a little extra oil. Cover and chill until required.

Place a ridged cast-iron frying pan over a high heat until you can feel the heat rising from the surface. Brush the tuna steaks with oil and place, oiled-side down, on the hot pan. Chargrill for 2 minutes.

Lightly brush the top side of the tuna steaks with a little more oil. Use a pair of tongs to turn the tuna steaks over, then season to taste with salt and pepper. Continue chargrilling for a further 2 minutes for rare or up to 4 minutes for well done.

Transfer the tuna steaks to serving plates and serve with the green sauce spooned over.

serves 4

3 tbsp olive oil

2 garlic cloves, chopped finely

10 anchovy fillets, drained and chopped

140 g/5 oz black olives, stoned and chopped

1 tbsp capers, rinsed

450 g/1 lb plum tomtoes, peeled, deseeded and chopped

pinch of cayenne pepper

salt

400 g/14 oz dried linguine

2 tbsp chopped fresh flat-leaf parsley, to garnish

linguine with anchovies, olives & capers

Heat the olive oil in a heavy-based saucepan. Add the garlic and cook over a low heat, stirring frequently, for 2 minutes. Add the anchovies and mash them to a pulp with a fork. Add the olives, capers and tomatoes and season to taste with cayenne pepper. Cover and simmer for 25 minutes.

Meanwhile, bring a saucepan of lightly salted water to the boil. Add the pasta, bring back to the boil and cook for 8–10 minutes, until tender, but still firm to the bite. Drain and transfer to a warmed serving dish.

Spoon the anchovy sauce into the dish and toss the pasta, using 2 large forks. Garnish with the parsley and serve immediately.

serves 4

600 g/1 lb 5 oz butternut
squash or pumpkin, peeled
and cut into bite-sized pieces

4 tbsp olive oil

1 tsp clear honey

25 g/1 oz fresh basil

25 g/1 oz fresh oregano

1 tbsp margarine

2 onions, finely chopped

450 g/1 lb arborio or other
risotto rice

175 ml/6 fl oz dry white wine

1.2 l itres/2 pints
hot vegetable stock

salt and pepper

roasted butternut squash risotto

Preheat the oven to 200°C/400°F/Gas Mark 6. Put the squash into a roasting tin. Mix 1 tablespoon of the oil with the honey and spoon over the squash. Turn the squash to coat it in the mixture. Roast in the preheated oven for 30–35 minutes, or until tender.

Meanwhile, put the basil and oregano into a food processor with 2 tablespoons of the remaining oil and process until finely chopped and blended. Set aside.

Heat the margarine and remaining oil in a large, heavy-based saucepan over a medium heat. Add the onions and fry, stirring occasionally, for 8 minutes, or until soft and golden. Add the rice and cook for 2 minutes, stirring to coat the grains in the oil mixture.

Pour in the wine and bring to the boil. Reduce the heat slightly and cook until the wine is almost absorbed. Add the stock, a little at a time, and cook over a medium-low heat, stirring constantly, for 20 minutes.

Gently stir in the herb oil and squash until thoroughly mixed into the rice and cook for a further 5 minutes, or until the rice is creamy and cooked but retaining a little bite in the centre of the grain. Season well with salt and pepper before serving.

makes 12

115 g/4 oz buckwheat flour

115 g/4 oz strong white
bread flour

7 g/¼ oz sachet easy-blend
dried yeast

1 tsp salt

375 ml/13 fl oz tepid milk

2 eggs, 1 whole and
1 separated

vegetable oil, for brushing

soured cream, smoked
salmon and lemon wedges,
to serve

pepper

blinis with smoked salmon

Sift both flours into a large, warmed bowl. Stir in the yeast and salt. Beat in the milk, whole egg and egg yolk until smooth. Cover the bowl and leave to stand in a warm place for 1 hour.

Place the egg white in a spotlessly clean bowl and whisk until soft peaks form. Fold into the batter. Brush a heavy-based frying pan with oil and set over a medium-high heat. When the frying pan is hot, pour enough of the batter onto the surface to make a blini about the size of a saucer.

When bubbles rise, turn the blini over with a palette knife and cook the other side until light brown. Wrap in a clean tea towel to keep warm while cooking the remainder. Serve the warm blinis with soured cream, smoked salmon, lemon wedges and season with black pepper.